(reading a burning book)

Also by Patrick Lawler

A Drowning Man Is Never Tall Enough

(reading a burning book)

by

Patrick Lawler

Patrick Lawler

BASFAL Books
Lima, Ohio

ACKNOWLEDGEMENTS

Sections of this book were first published in the following magazines and journals:

(sleep)	*Nimrod* (finalist in the Pablo Neruda Prize)
(breath)	*The Lowell Review*
(water)	*Central Park*
(death)	*Gopherwood Review*
(food)	*Central Park*
(light)	*Red Brick Review*
(dreams)	*American Letters & Commentary* and *Wayne Literary Review*

Published by BASFAL Books
517 S. Main Street
P.O. Box 4503
Lima, OH, 45802-4503

Cover photograph by Andrew Selvagio.
Cover design by Dan Jankowski.

Library of Congress Cataloging-in-Publication Data

Lawler, Patrick.
    Reading a burning book : a booklength poem / Patrick Lawler.
        p.   cm.
    ISBN 0-7880-0146-9
    I. Title.
    PS3562.A867R43   1994
    811'.54--dc20   94-10582
                                                               CIP

For my mother Ann, my wife Janet, my daughter Nicole.
To the woman who gave me life, who gives me life, who shows me life.

A special thanks to Bob, Tim, and Fran.

TABLE OF CONTENTS

(sleep)   1

(silence)   15

(breath)   23

(words)   31

(water)   47

(death)   57

(food)   63

(love)   71

(light)   81

(dreams)   91

(sleep)

> We share a world when we are awake; each
> sleeper is in a world of his own.
>   Herakleitos

(My father,
Schooled in the art of sleeping,
Slept. A narcoleptic, he would doze off
At the drop of anything, at the drop
Of a snowflake, at the drop
Of his slow gray hat.

He slept through the depression
While other men floated out of ten-story windows.
He slept through Normandy Beach.
He slept through my sister's ringlets,
My mother's villenelles, the unfinished

Crossword puzzles of our conversations.
Through Eisenhower and Sputnik,
He crumbled up beneath his hat.

Sleep fell around him. It spilled out
Of his shoes, out of his coat's big pockets.
He left it behind in his footsteps.
One saw it in the brittle eyes
Of chickens when he passed. One heard it
In the stomach of a cat. One thought
Of it when reading Chekhov.

Whenever I saw the color black,
It was my father sleeping.)

What is most *to be feared* is insomnia. The doctor has
not spoken to me about it, nor have I spoken of it to
him. But I am fighting it myself by a very, very
strong dose of camphor in my pillow and mattress.

Van Gogh

(I can't sleep.
A wounded man is in the garden.
We have peered into the grave
Formed by his hands, the glaze of his late
Eyes. We must notify someone.

Try a bath of Lime Flower, a sachet
Of chamomile. The Countess of Soissons
Even had cushions for her thumbs.

Drink sweet marjoram, hawthorn, and melissa.

No.

There is a strange light,
The sunset draining away
Over Cross Lake.

Sometimes we see everything clearly:
The magpie's nest in a tall acacia,
The sunflower in its false fever, the dull

Orange of the freshly cut earth.
An avenue of pink flowering chestnuts.

4

Yet we mustn't let clarity deceive.
The wounded man dreams of our demise,
Does the dance of our departure.)

No small art is it to sleep: it is necessary to keep
awake all day for that purpose.
                                                        Nietzsche

(All wrong from the start, I began
By separating what is from what is,
Wondering in unearned astonishment.
I live lavishly off what is lost.

My father sleeps in his dark suits;
My mother walks in a pink

Haze. It is late at night,
And I am reading Nietzsche, his quest
For the depth
Of God.

My brother and sisters talk
In their blue sleep, a chorus
Of nonsense and light, their voices
Moving like incest
From bedroom to bedroom.

All day my father reads the burning
Book; all night he writes it.

Nietzsche had his tray of sedatives
Against his insomnia: Chloral hydrate
And Veronal. What keeps the words
Coming? The dialogue
Winds through the thick night air.

The solipsist sleeps.
I keep whispering a word until
It grows smaller and smaller.)

> Nothing frightens me more than the false serenity
> of a sleeping face.
> Cocteau

(There is a story
Here somewhere, but I won't
Let it out.

My mother would rub herself with essence
Of benzoin; she would scent her sheets
With orange blossom, heliotrope and
Oil of bergamot. Still she would
Sleepwalk in her pink flannel gown.

My mother descends the octave
Of stairs, a crucifix hanging
From her neck,
Settling between her breasts—
The round heads of the silver
Nails delicately driven.)

6

But, speaking of "resemblances," I mean that dream presentations are analogous to the forms reflected in water, as indeed we have already stated. In the latter case, if motion in the water be great, the reflexion has no resemblance to its original, nor do the forms resemble the real objects. Skillful, indeed, would he be in interpreting such reflexions who could rapidly discern, and at a glance comprehend, the scattered and distorted fragments of such forms, so as to perceive that one of them represents a man, or a horse, or anything whatever.

Aristotle

(Places my father did not sleep:
Greece and Rangoon. Moscow. Madrid.
He did not sleep
In Vancouver or Martinique.

He never snored
In the musical air of Helsinki.

Trapped in his geography, he moved
Along the rich black borders of sleep,
Guided by those first cartographers,
Who found emptiness in all the wrong places,
Who created the world out of chasms
And crossroads. When they stopped

Dreaming, there was the air's edge.
My father did not fall asleep in Africa.
He did not fall asleep in Dublin
Though he wished he had.

It does not seem possible:
I find the world everywhere.
Here is a man. There is a horse.
This is anything whatever.)

People are not going/ To dream of baboons and
periwinkles./ Only, here and there, an old sailor,/
Drunk and asleep in his boots,/ Catches tigers/
In red weather.

                                        Wallace Stevens

(My father understood the sleep of animals.
A crow is the stone of sleep. Coal
Is the bird of sleep. This is life.

This is life.

The crocodiles open up like car
Hoods; the elephants are the color
Of dented garbage cans.
The spigots of the birds' necks
Whistle over the emptiness.
This is life. This is life.
A cross old bass. Trout
Sleeping like the throats of women.
The breath of black bees.

Listen to the parrot wondering
If this is Africa. The green gum
In its veins wonders.
Look, the crocodiles sleep like sneakers.
Something is rocking inside them.
The heart. The heart is almost

Extinct. My mother's sleep turns into snow;
My father's sleep turns into nothing.

Glub. Glub.
The hippopotamus walks like
A diplomat with a secret mission.)

8

My dreams are not me; they are not Nature, or the
Not-me: they are both. They have a double conscious-
ness, at once sub- and ob-jective.
                                        Emerson

(It is a regular dream with the usual
Things happening. Europe is sleeping
On trains. Men are wearing sleeve garters.
Women sweep past the closed
Doors of the Pullman cars.

The body of a train conductor:
Ticket stubs clenched in his hands.

Then Freud shows up
Out of one of his dreams.
The barber pole spins its slow blood.
The lotions, the clippers, the cannisters
Of combs. He looks haggard—
His coat like a dusty road.

Then I am sitting in a red chair,
The color of bad blood.
The white sheet snaps stormily.
Bottles of liquid like green secrets.
Chunky shaving mugs. The snick
Of scissors around my ears.

There's a sign over the mirror.

Someone, hunched and uncertain, walks
Through the door, but the bell doesn't
Ting. A mistake has been made.
Even when dead, Laius lives.)

In a strange room you must empty yourself for sleep.
And before you are emptied for sleep, what are you. And
when you are emptied for sleep, you are not. And when
you are filled with sleep, you never were. I don't know
what I am. I don't know if I am or not.

Faulkner

(This is the poem my mother walks through,
The poem my father sleeps through.
I think it was Kepler who discovered
The way the moon hooks into the darkness.

My father would have taught
Me that, if he hadn't had his own
Crosspurposes, his own
Black world to step back into.

I squeeze my eyes until all that remains
Of the night is the night's dark juices.
I took this method from my father
As I watched his knotted breath,
The scratched air around his body.
Is is also was.
He slept through Cantigny and Belleau
Wood; he slept through gilt-edged securities,
The Teapot Dome, and Al Capone.
He slept through the landing
Of Lindbergh at Le Bourget airdrome.
He slept through the moon

That hung over Hanoi.)

Our life is two-fold: Sleep hath its own world,/ A
boundary between the things misnamed/ Death and
existence; Sleep hath its own world,/ And a wide realm
of wild reality.

Byron

(During the moonwalk when my father was sleeping,
My mother applauded. She watched the astronauts
Chug along in their puffy gray suits. They'd almost
Drift off in a lazy leap as if nothing could
Hold them. Then they'd return and suddenly stick.

It was late at night, the voices of my brother
And sisters winding blue through the air. My father
Woke and called me. The air was blue and
False and blue. It was as if he were lying
In a hole. The moon was glued to the windows.

If I had taken one step in any direction, I would have drifted away.)

> The sleeper turns into himself and falls back into the
> womb.
>
> Roheim

(First the sky is the sky.
It is always in the middle of itself.
Storm clouds or clearing.
Scarred with light. Simply scared.
Some things that happen do.
And some things that happen don't.

For example, what we have scraped
Together, dream scraps for genitals,
Dream scraps for hearts,
An uncle's pocket watch
Like a testicle that has stopped.

The doctor arrives with bad news
On his breath. My mother carries
The color blue inside her womb.
Fear: someone will be listening

And I'll have nothing to say.

It is always 3 A.M.
Time: a tower falling toward us
In the dark.)

He giveth his beloved sleep.
Psalms 127:2

(The wounded man is in the garden.
At first we ignored him, mistaking
His wounds for geraniums.
My wife says we should call someone.
He is turning blue among the flowers'
Crushed throats, the petals
Like scalded flesh, his hands

Twisted in ivy. My wife cannot sleep
Thinking how beautiful
He is becoming. But the garden
Is turning into weeds because she
Can't bear to enter it.
Dandelions and clover. Thistle.
Black Medic. Chickweed. Oxalis.
Yellow Rocket, Veronica, Violets.

I need to enter the names
Of things. I want the word
For the weed that grows
Out of my heart.)

> A sense of real things comes doubly strong.
> Keats

(Cross Lake is flickering with sunset.
I am watching the hat of a man
Who is burning. My father sleeps
In a different language. Now he sleeps
In Latin; sometimes he sleeps

In German—the dark cloud of his snoring.

I need to make the visible invisible
Again, so I can see it. Behind me
There are centuries of sleeping.
I am sleeping through Galileo's stars.

I am sleeping through
Paracelsus, Hippocrates, and Newton.
The sixth century sleeps in its own smoke.
The twelfth century sleeps like a monk.
It wonders what God is
For.

The full moon: night's ovulation.)

> Even sleeping men are doing the world's business
> and helping it along.
> Herakleitos

(I am watching a bird rising over
Cross Lake, moving in tight circles.
It has relinquished its mind,
It has abandoned its stumbling logic.

My father is sealed in his sleeping,
Holding onto each ember of pain,
Fearing that nothing else is real.

He inhales and he is part world;
He exhales and it is part him.

My mother, pink and cautious, walks
Along the shore. Her sleep cannot
Contain her. She still knows the dance of air.

And my mother burns
The burning book,
And by that light
We love her.

My wife's body is under a blue sheet,
A wave that won't go by.
My daughter rocks in my arms.
To have a language for less,
To have a music for leaving.

I am losing all ambition: the bird
Pronounces the word sky with its body.)

(silence)

Now the Sirens have a still more fatal weapon than their
song, namely their silence. And though admittedly it is
as conceivable that someone might possibly have escaped
from their singing; but from their silence certainly never.
Franz Kafka

What we cannot speak about we must pass over in silence.
Ludwig Wittgenstein

...we must choose between beauty and silence.
Susan Griffin

White
City:

White
Noise:

This will have to do: snow falls in the mountains
as if it were snowing. The point: to stand perfectly still
and let the world fall around you, to stand still
in the loosening air. This is what the world wants.

Silence: I am talking down the hole
                                        of death

White
Dreams:

A clearing in the woods. This fleshy, sleeping place
full of puffballs, nine or ten planets, ball-shaped
fruiting bodies with white punchy skin.

I'm not
saying anything

                    that you wouldn't
        say   if   you
                    were
    me.   I'm   not   saying anything...

Broken into, they release their spores. Ancient.
Anointed. They rise out of nothing. The dark juice,
the pulp of our bodies. Silence.

                mansions of silence
                distractions

The day the birds walked off the sky. Silence.
I drag out the pictures to fill in the skips. The male's body
is mute; the female's body speaks the silence.

            I
        am being absorbed

      by   silence.

                                  it is radiant.
        it   circulates
                    among us.

This is the gazebo full of folding chairs and sunlight;
the tuba, a gentleman bent over his golden accounts.

    I   keep   looking
                        but
                the
                           air
                gets   in
    the way.

The sailors and waitresses that surround me, the snapshots
of Florida, the smudge pots burning all night in the
orange groves. The egrets stand like guilt. I am not
my life.

      fiery, flickery, migraine-like,

            the horn player
            watches her whole self
            come out
            the other end.

Statues leak sleep. Rooms full of it. The cathedral is torn
down. The wrecking ball breaks the columns like aged
bones. Dust on the mouth of the statue.

        words   wrap
        around everything.

              hide everything
              in their gauze.

        flesh:
        music.

We wear our cracks aptly. At night we are ice, transparent,
thick, scarred. Dreams slip blue beneath us. A mirror
is held at the bottom of our lives. It can't be helped:
the something we leave behind, the nothing we step into.

silence is oppression.   silence
                                    is

                        a

                                                    strategy
                    to recognize   oppression.

            White
            Wind:
                                White

                                Dress:

People with their faces smashed against the lens of a
camera. Nothing is real unless we have two of it.
Timeless images of elephants and umbrellas. Silence.

                    shattered clothes
                        posthumous   chairs

                                        a dead bird
                            is   flying
                                        into the ground

When I go to the mailbox, it is as if I were watching
a great current at the point where it has stopped.

Silence: I am
                                        speaking
                                            into death.

20

God is changeless, omniscient, self-subsistent, and not-real.
The last fact he loves the most. Light writes its silence
on his terrible body.

                              no   sky
                                   no sun
                              no   emptiness

Copious. Connected. Perfect white heads think the wholeness
that dreamily develops around them. They dream the lush
dark world that denies them. Thinking.

                         touch words
                                  with
                                        torches.
                  silence: the burning book
                                        reads itself.

The structures of the world—silent. The martyrs to the acquisition
of knowledge—silent. The desire to see into stone: the fossils
almost luminous, swimming in ludic light.

                                               the songs
                                               all over
                                               the body

Silence: walking into a roomful of sleepers. Silence: the sound
of what is stolen from us. Silence: the seduction,
the burglary of hope.

                  this   I
                       is
                         between
                  selves.

Shackles of sound. Science. Seance. Culture: the voice
that has been taken out of the victim.

                                        Listen
                        to the

                        silence   on
            the other   side

                                of this
            poem.

Words talking to words in a world of words. If you
keep reading this, you will vanish. The silence will
swallow you up.

                        quest-

            ion

Another silence: Fountain of flesh: Snow: A star you carry
in your ear: A fish floating in stone: A puffball: white
planet: white thought.

                silence:

        words inhaling.

(breath)

First Wind: I would like to
know what it is
I am saying then
I would just say
the thing I am
saying and I wouldn't
have to go through

this. And he said:
It's not necessary. I'm
standing in a false
country. And there
are these factories:
factories for memory,
for pain, visions,

love, blood; factories for
our wondering stretched between
false machines. My voice silver-thin,
a dead star, moist
in her ear. What
would the Virgin's breasts
have tasted like?

Inspiration? Light? It is as
if someone dragged an
orchestra into a desert.
And he said: Yes. It's
all whiteness and thick
air, tissues of golden
air. And I listen

for those sounds like
the electric movements of
a cat. And I have
collected my childhood and
turned it into a
burnt thing. I walk
carefully as if the air

would scar me.
The desert has its
oily light, its factories
of belief, of abstract
politics, of roses, of rain.
How can saints live
with the constant hum

of their own bodies?
He said: I have
come to relish,
to drink, to stir.
I have come to relieve
you. She said: how
cold it is

to continue. And yet
there is the first self.
My body hums
beneath her touch.
I lay this burnt thing
at her feet—
the thing I am saying.

Second Wind: It is as if the air
were an idea. And
she said the words
were here first. And
she said I am my
own oxygen turning
flame blue. We are

in over our heads.
And this thing I am
saying won't go away.
We conspire. How can we
find this thing which will
reconnect us to our hearts?
And she said: we are

our hearts. The light inside
her is blinking wildly;
she wants the bare maximum.
I look into the
limelight of the machine,
the brain of the
machine. Nothing will ever

die here. She said the
burning
book is full of visions, truths.
She said the burning book
is full of lies.
It depends on whether
after having burned it
it burns your eyes.

The light is played
like an instrument. And
she said: Imagine my breath
filling your body.
The music is a stranger
seated in a
shattered house. The musical

instruments are breathing
in the heat, breathing out
the cool lining of the throat.
Like dismembered angels
parts of bodies are blowing
out the other
ends of horns.

I am back
in the desert, the brass
turned into sun, the flames
on the strings, the
nuclear light from the
tuba. She said: how can
I divide my breath

from the air? We listen
to the intermittent music
of our sex, to this
thing we can't be saying

27

but keep saying as
if the words are all that keep
the stars in place.

Third Wind: I have to catch
my death. And he said:
I am looking for
you. His eyes snarled.
I drag all the sky
down into my lungs. I
am trying to talk

myself out of this.
I'm playing with
these death toys, the
dark secretions from the
machines. I have all
these words that won't
fit together, no matter

what. "Wind," she says.
"Touch. Thought." "Silence," he
says. "Hot silence." I
am in a liquid
dream and nothing is
dissolving. These sounds: pieces
of air. I let

the breath out of
each word. She says,
"The insomnia of things.
The fever of things."
"It's not necessary,"
he replies. She says,
"We can walk on music

if we're careful."
The communists are crying;
Hegel is climbing
into his invisible car.
Capitalists bury us in making.
I am swallowing my own death,
my fears, the

diamond of my desire.
It is as if
our way of seeing
were burning up around
us. He says, "The
oily light of the
desert." She says, "The

pristine light of the
desert." The thing I am saying
gets in my way. Air builds
its house inside me. I
am a musical thing.
I am a burnt thing.
"Talk," she says. "Talk."

(words)

...you can love a name and if you love a name then
saying that name any number of times only makes you
love it more, more violently more persistently more
tormentedly.

Gertrude Stein

Poetry
Forgive me for having helped you understand
you're not made of words alone.

Roque Dalton

chiasma (ki-az'me) n., pl.

1. Anatomy. A crossing or intersection of two tracts, as of nerves or
    ligaments.

the train proceeds   on   horizontal ladder

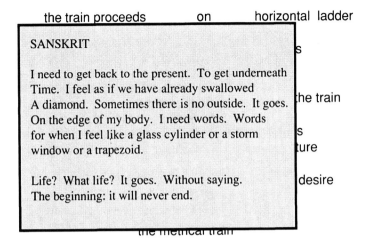

SANSKRIT

I need to get back to the present. To get underneath
Time. I feel as if we have already swallowed
A diamond. Sometimes there is no outside. It goes.
On the edge of my body. I need words. Words
for when I feel like a glass cylinder or a storm
window or a trapezoid.

Life? What life? It goes. Without saying.
The beginning: it will never end.

s

he train

s

ture

desire

the metrical train

Marx and Freud sleeping in their compartments
        "I   want
                    to get off now."

Einstein's train
    2. Genetics. A point of contact between homologous chromosomes,
considered the cytological manifestation of crossing over.

                    the etymology of the word   penetralia
        the vatic
            voice of the train

        the diamonded declarations
                "I travel light"
    (by the word travel you will see
    a picture of the word light)
            the entropic train

            perfect lucidity
                unravelling
        to dismantle the literary   the literal
            the oppressive
    with a yelp   a bawl   a chuckle

            libre/ration

VIETNAMESE

What to do with all the words in dictionaries?
                        Archaic words.
                        Obsolete.
Words that have forgotten what the throat feels like.

Despised words. We occupy the world with our words.

Words that are the enemy of words.

How we try to keep people without words.
New words flickering--holographic.

a verb is a word

  an action

    a state
a being

   either physical

or mental

   Chomsky's train

rides through the blue hills

of sentences

  "what is"

   vs. "what is"

  a link

CREE

Hermits are traveling and they stop a Cree to ask for directions.
He tells them they must travel "Two porcupines to the north."

Words like a cocoon
with everything inside them.
Or words

like a stream weaving through fingers.

   Direction and distance (porcupines
dwell in areas 3-4 miles). But the Cree also gives them
the trees they will see, the birch, the vegetation,
the animals. He brings the earth into his language.

"Still, my words lose me."

My mouth wide open and things flying in to replace me.

BEKOS

Psammetichos, an Egyptian Pharaoh, was after the original
language, so he raised babies in silent chambers.

Blue rooms. He thought he heard the word bekos, which
is the Phrygian word for bread.

Originally the world spoke bekos.

Imagine a language that would conveniently turn into things.
Say the word berry and feel it pressed to your lips, its
flesh, in slow motion, punctured by teeth.

The perfect language--a one word language where
the word for death is the word for love.

install an electric

current in your heart

34

sex
dangles from
her earlobes

   the
    of

fantasy:
   masturb

to the mus
Glass

  she cares
his heart

a spark in th
of a tremblin

    bee

flower

GAELIC

Eventually even the river loses itself under the bridges
of Dublin.

The rose of you--
Dark and dormant, tingly.

We carry each other's language.
You are the past tense of me.
Part words. Part body.

When we are separated, I discover the smells of you
on different parts of me. When we touch,
I am afraid we will burn holes in each other.

Tell me.

When we're together the world is complete, just as it is--
Brilliantly, there is its beginning all around us,
And wisely, there is everything necessary for its end.

---

body-

sap

fall into
poems

at each other's hearts
a rag fire in the loins

  she nourishes

saucers
fires
spoonfuls of sparks

   lighting
her mouth

as she sips

GREEK

Tell me the word.
Free and flowering. Or claustrophobic. Tell me the word.
Candlelight, rain, yellow, shiver, miffed, sleep, death, throat.

When I am the rain, I sing just like the rain.
Sometimes the woman I am loving is Clytemnestra. We
are yearning for another time, further back than the past.

Bring back the gods that presided over
          emptiness
          reason
          lust.
Let's see what they can do.

For you I am retrieving everything: Music for
Miscellaneous Saints. Ideas for the Void.
I stand in the sterile sunlight of each word.

And we remember Clytemnestra,
          her crazy green song.

---

it is inconceivable that I am not you

Romany is a   spoken   sea

see   words as   wandering

      (the Nazis murdered) 500,000 Rom
the gas chambers
            glowed in fantastic
      (If you ask a dozen   gypsies the same

     question,

    Adrienne Rich is riding
      a train through Africa
discovering a language
    it is the only train
    out of her

SWAHILI
This language is all apricot and pink, Smoke darkening, growing fat And sweet, ready to be discovered. "Your voice is the color of the earth, of the leaves As they touch the earth. Your breath is a ruby. Parts of you are crimson, parts of you are plum.

       you get a dozen

    different
answers.
    If you ask one gypsy the same question a dozen times, you will still

get a dozen different answers.
    marime means

   defilement   the demarcati

   of the human body

    the upper and lower halve
must never mix

the Rom are living in an alien

 they wander
   like words

the two halves of the world
touching
     the fantastic

ROMANY
"We sit on the deck reading Shelley and Keats. Then the Hungarian rain touches our necks. And for a moment we aren't here and that makes things right or nearly so. (I am riding this animal inside me and it is blind but I don't tell you.) "We sit on the deck reading Burns and Blake, Questioning the rose. It is, as we suspected, Spiraling inside its crimson self. We need a language we can love each other in." A new geography: The lush gullies, A harvest of roses, Words locked inside. "I burn to ride the waters of you. Your ecstasy: miles of it."

all her   life

          she wanted

to be
a russian
novel
      Dostoyevsky's train

        is full of snow

SIGN
 	
Words choreographed.   Words inhabiting space.
           Body-words.
A river of words
                 flow
                 from
                 the
                 hand.
Words that take up the space between us.
Mouth mother. The mouth that wraps itself
 	
           around the earth.

to take place in st. petersburg
        to be a description

    of snow
        falling
         fantasy: making love under a snow

   filled sky

     on an old man's sho[e]

a chuckle   of ruble[s]

    the long white   glove

floats down the volga

    I am writing my first

russian novel

   vaslov says that it is in

RUSSIAN Children are writing poems to the distance of their mothers' eyes. We need a place to call home. Anger bursts behind the blood-red barns. The snowy fields. We carry around the memory of smoke, faces burning in every window. You see, the dead lie down inside history--along side the living. There are other possibilities. Sure. Remember childhood. Language like a translucent container. Or adolescence. When it was pungent and amber and oblong and fat. "I ask over and over: what can we do to save ourselves? Now. Now. Now." "And I touch my lover, the benevolence of her breasts, her hand, her stark hair. Terrified, we dance, swirling the pigments of our bodies around in the air."

no danger of being   read   freedom

mea culpa
mea culpa

         may a coup

'open

      projections on a screen

     may a couple

   may a couple

     how lonely the road inside Descartes' head
don't look at what I am doing
   the world full of quilt

    he leaves his head and he is   gone

sky-silver
bird road
  the road you put in your

   the road a bird

     the road the travele

   takes to the other side

of the brain

  a bird falls out of Descar

   dream

on the other side
of the brain is the

   on the other side
   of the body
   is the mind
   an egg filled
   with bright
   green liquid

SPANISH

I detect my own death inside your stories. Can I touch it?

LATIN

We build this church of words around us. Always the things
that are not there. Everywhere I look I see them.
Trembling.

With beautiful aqua eyes,
The dead keep trying to stay dead.
We admire their persistence, their cruel logic.

Aquinas had his distinction between body and soul. Put simply
it is this: The soul is a piece of glass the body swallows.

That's all.

When I walk into libraries, I feel myself being swallowed
by books. I become nothing but words. Agricula.
Agriculorum.

"Still I am trying to find out what will keep us awake.
        Something amazing?
        A stone walking inside itself?
        Or just plain facts?"

"I wonder how my life would look with a door in it,
with the light touching it,
with the world on the other side of it."

38

Why wouldst

thou be a   breeder of
words words   words

KHOI-KHOIN

Staccato clicks and clacks. A boutique of sound.
This language is spoken by breathing in. So you bring the world
through the crack of the mouth to form the sound.
Bright words. Cut words. World inside them.
        Illuminating.
Read to me
the burning book of the body--each word's small fire.

                    wordslap
you   would   pluck out

          the heart
of my   mystery

to post with such dexterity to incestuous sheets within the book and volume of my brain

to put an antic
          disposition on   may

sweep   to my

DANISH

"I have made up my mind about Death.
It doesn't exist

Outside me." Reading the prisons,

Reading the windows, reading the stains on the walls
        of the skin.
Reading what the stars leave behind on the water.
Reading what the silence leaves behind

          after it has used up the words.

          dram of

I know
not seems
the time
          is out of

not walk in the

words words words quintessence

of dust   I know a   hawk the
    conscience is the   question

that's a fair   thought to lie   between words   words words

sing for me
          Aphasia
vinter   words

KHOISAN

the outside of words
the inside of words
the rituals we make with our mouths

"deathenated"

neologisms

she writes her science

          her   fictions
     her fantastic

               Narcissus

is buried in his   mirror

                                        Echolalia
                                        sing for
                                        me

          she carries her egg
          she carries her egg filled with light

"Henry III of France
     became terrified   at the sight of eggs"

          she carrie ARABIC

                        The mural in the mouth
                        I watch my heartbeat in the sun

he carries an egg with a map inside
                        This book swallows all other books
                        Your mouth swallows my mouth

                        The funeral of words
          she carries an egg   The arena of struggle

with Henry III inside
                                        words are cracks
                                             cracks

we will be back after this message

ENGLISH

A word is growing inside me.

A word
is being
pulled
through
me.

his

the dead "I"   to the death kingdom

this book

re you believe
saying

I will not entertain you any longer I will sell you the hole you will fall through

I will sell you the "faute de mieux"

the analecta of desire

will sell you

the unlinkable

a dolphin arcing
a monkey

I will
sell you mystification
the iris of the eye   the crisis of the I

YIDDISH

Those who control words control memory.
Those who control memory control history.
Those who control history control our lives.

I'm thinking in one language. I'm writing
in another.

I dream in a third language.

I am armed with words.

burning

ld

hronicles

te begins sending
me

burn
his
book

now

41

was down

today in active

              John Jacob Astor's train

is transparent

        trading
        the yen   and

the german mark   were down

the pound was down today

            golden

> ## WHISTLE LANGUAGE OF KUSKOY
>
> Secret languages.
> Colonial languages.
> Lexicons of violence.
>
> "Hey, Flaubert, who do you think you are?"
>
> My dreams are burnholes. Babble.
> The pigmentation of words.
>
> Can you teach me your language?

        Ezra

his train

frozen

      gold closed

    fantasy: a shimmering creature

a man dressed in a garter belt
      today down

        to last
        dream

today we are down

    to the last   vibrations of

    the day closed
      with a gold

> ## ESPERANTO
>
> Words can turn
> Us into things.
> The economy
> Of words.
>
> "OK, what language do I write in? What language do I dream in?"
>
> "I am made for words."

spilling   all
      over

  the   place
      a gold drip

    a pocket watch bleeding

heart-earned

once   a time
there was

the
        cut

into his wife

        times

    there was
no eating

CHINESE

First, I am not my life.... it's there, like everything
else, it is bulky; it is outside me. I can touch it
but it kinda moves away.

Listen.

Think of the way life inhabits an object. The physicality.
Remember details, shapes, sizes. Dig deep into the actual
while remaining on the surface. That's the trick. Remember.
Breast thigh trout butter. This is the truth. The Cathedral
of Erotic Misery, etc. etc.

Not really.

I'm blending into the world around me. Words?
How do I say this in Chinese?

no eating   the house
no eating the body   of the mother
    her breasts were made of   coffin wood

they scattered every step

            the birds had eaten   away the sky
    eating   was   everywhere
the trains never stopped   in the dusty   towns

    nibble nibble old old woman   hobbling on a stick
    strawberries cream beds like the breasts of birds

ITALIAN

"Next to an Italian stream, under an Italian sky,
I gorge myself on the light in your eyes."

Tell me the word.
When you are in it, time is.
Time is voluptuous. The air around
me smells of you.

I can wear it.

for a finger the fire in the oven

fall through the holes in your body
    into your own

    mommy
            give

    coherence
magnificent mouth

43

before he died the father believed every word

logopoeia   I'm

listening

to the flesh radio

and it says:

PORTUGUESE

After the Portuguese formally ended slave trafficking,
the slave traders continued for over two centuries
because slave traders simply renamed the raids "rescue missions."

Words
have a way
of capturing people.

So do images. So does history.

In the rich dark lagoon of language,
We meet our monsters.

they burn
the villages

they burn the books

it asks:
is anyone listening

barriers to fulfillment
Freud: the father figure projected by the unconscious mind
Marx: the father figure projected by culture

social   and   psychic   revolution   are   the   same

fantasy:

the woman I love prepare[s]
she shows me how to mo[ve]
like silk she shows me
how to be velvet she sho[ws]
how to turn my lips
into the color of dark berri[es]
logy-poe[try]

HINDUSTANI

I need the language of the future (Glow-words. People-words.
Gold-words.) Of sleep (Diamond-words. Missing-words.). Of struggle
(Earth-words. Water-words. Blood-words.) Of love
(Rose-words. Hot-words. Wind-words. Vaginal-words.). Healing
words. Words that rise in the smoke of the burning book (Sky-
words). A language of change. Words that work. Words of the gold
bee. Post-Hiroshima words. Post-Auschwitz words. Post
words. A lamp is a language with desire floating inside.
Or something like that.

Lacan's train moves fr[om]
the imaginary
to

the symbolic

one way to get rid
of   the dying   father

is to become the mother

44

ESKIMO   uly wondrous

Holophrastic.

Some words connect with stars, sweeten the mouth, taste
like licked music.

Some words damage.
Look at how we say the world.
Alienated. Fragmented. Hierarchical. World as possessed.
Words as objects, as distance.

Sometimes a word will forget there are other words.

I want to walk with you
Where all these words for snow fall through the sky.

a holographic
self
staring back at us
          with pearly eyes   and a fiery   mouth
                a chiasmatic   self

          the nothing
             train stops
             here

          the last things

burn this book

          anything

     it is
          saying
          something
     more intelligent
than us is singing

          never yet
was put into words

          this burning

WHALE

I want to take you where the humpback lives--a blue
world of blue sound.
Church organs bulge under water.
Sisters of a weird, intelligent choir.

Someone blowing across a bottle: a fluttering, a booming,
a lump in the throat of the sea.

Echolocation:poets who use voices
                to find out

                  where we are.
We listen to the mystic language, the sonar lovemaking
between the whale mother and her calf.
Their way of seeing the world is also their way of saying the world.

Their voice is a lamp.
We swim between their conversations.
Our words. Strange words. We wonder what we're saying.

(water)

This is the poem
written with burnt
fingers. This is the
wind inside the
wind turning the
pages of the
burning book.

The daughter sings to fish. The silver brains of fish become the water. The woman stands on the opposite shore playing with her translucent fingers. The puzzle pieces: the twisted coral of the brain or the crystalline knowing flesh. She does not see the man who is watching a body burning on another shore. (See figure 1.)

Figure 1. Photo of light

This is the poem
that remembers
everything. This
is the poem that
remembers
nothing.

Jacques Cousteau says to study a fish you must become a fish. You must spin through the soundless towns, the serious cities beneath the water. You must cruise to the spot where quietly blackness is brewed. Your body must become a language: the fish are made from vowels. (See figure 2.)

Figure 2. Controlling Metaphor

This is the
poem where
the self is
murdered.
This is the
poem where

the   father
opens   the
door.

  The fish at the bottom of the sea: the darkness turns their thoughts to ink. Eyes crushed. The snipe eel waves the flag of its body, surrendering to itself. The hatchet fish wears its costume of scars. The lantern fish, its body swaying, flips past its own light into the clumsy dark. (See figure 3.)

Figure 3. Window

This is the poem
Byron
wrote when he
watched
Keats' body
burning. These are
the words
VirginiaWoolf left
behind as her body
drifted downward
with its death
pearls.

Afraid of the greed of the gold brain, the logic machines, the locks of light, dissipation; afraid of the father eyes, lonely and fierce; the suicide poet opens the door of the grave. Water is the only thing inhabitable, at least for the mind. "I am afraid of here," the woman said, and couldn't leave. Sealed off, preserved under water. Stars filling up the ocean. It is possible to imagine all that has to pass through us to be real, to be palatable, to be what is the flaming present. (See figure 4.)

Figure 4. The Door the Father Walks Through

This is the
poem that will
float. This is
the poem that
will not float.
This is the will
not to be a
poem.

While the body burned and the book burned, Byron went swimming off the shores of Viareggio, far from the scratching at the heart, far from the imaginary cities where imaginary women wear lingerie like butterflies caught in fans, far from the epicurean fruit, the cousin, the countess. As if he swallowed by mistake the breath of a saint, he shed his weight. (See figure 5.)

Figure 5. "I wear another I."

This is the poem
where the father
says he is doing
it for our own
good. This is the
poem where the
father vanishes.

He moved like failure among flowers, effortlessly. He moved like a wedding of acrobats. Then the green water went fat. Flesh was made flesh; he closed his plum-heavy eyes. Transcendence and tragedy: those old themes. Words are not worth it unless they float. (See figure 6.)

Figure 6. Map of the Original World

This is the poem
wrapped in the
skin of a fish.

This   is   the
poem wearing
its words to a
funeral.

The woman stands on the opposite shore. She is remembering the
ceremonies of faithlessness. She is remembering the self-possessed. She
is remembering how as a child she would curl up in the hole she kept
inside herself. She reads her life by the sweetness of the burning body.
(See figure 7.)

Figure 7. Children Rising to the Surface

This   is   the
poem with the
hole   in   it.
This   is   the
poem we fall
through.

The water that shuffles behind is guided back by the burst jewel of the
body, the screaming of the bird, the closing book. A little more distance—
farther out. We know when it's over: the water stumbles the moment it
becomes the shore. (See figure 8.)

Figure 8. The Absent Poet

This   is   the
poem   that
cannot   be
written. This
is the poem
where you say
goodbye to the
self.

Of course, we need to swim through time in order to return to the scene of our origins. Look at Nietzsche, Marx, and Heidegger. Their big burning clocks light the insides of their pockets. (See figure 9.)

Figure 9. Voices of Fish

This is the
poem made of
water. Water
is the dialogue
between earth
and air.

"I never know what to do with the self. I keep writing and it is like removing a dead animal from my heart. And the static tears up the air." "And women are dying inside these beautiful machines men have built for them." "I keep writing and it is like saying, 'C'mon, get up.'" "It is as if I am building my own necessary death out of words." (See figure 10.)

Figure 10. The Evidence

This is the
poem with
dream fish
and voices.
This is the
poem with a
boy who has
lost his brain.

The flood destroyed all shores, all boundaries. The water entered the houses, the shops. Furniture and lamps drifted. The water seeped into the funeral home; caskets floated past us. We clung to Queequeg's coffin. We died the very same moment we were being born. The fish sewed themselves into the water. The world settled beneath the blue jewel. (See figure 11.)

Figure 11. Around Everything is a Music

This is the
world floating
on the surface
of the poem.
These are the
rain   pools
women carry
inside them.

Every night Leander swam to the opposite shore to see Hero. He was guided by the torch she set blazing on top of a tower. One stormy night, the light was blown out by the wind and Leander perished. His heart fell through the water like a stone. (See figure 12.)

Figure 12. The Only Way Out of Here

This is the
poem where
the star fish
catches fire.
This is the
poem a fish
carries in his
brain.

The woman who stands on the opposite shore is ready to dive into the blue heart of the sea, into her own blue remembering, into her own blue imagining. Star fire burns in a star fish. The water is a lung she is falling through. Time-parent. Woman reading the water, reading the fish, eating the dreams of fish. Things that come toward her out of sleep, covered in algae. Dream-parent. (See figure 13.)

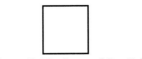

Figure 13. The Scene of Our Origins

This is the
poem where
the father,
after climbing
the stair with
those terrible
footsteps, dies.
This is the
poem the
daughter puts
her hand in.
This is the
water she is
reading. This
is the lake like
dead crystal.
This is the
mind of a fish.

The woman on the opposite shore carries Keats' burning body like a memory to her window. She lugs it to the tower. Its spools of light unfolding. The light from the burning body spilling on the water like moonbeams, like new breast milk. The sea is the sea because it does not think it is the sea. Flesh-parent. Leander stumbles, chokes on the big gulps of light, touches the heartbeat of fish. Thoughts like silver leaping into her eyes, Hero sees nothing but water and light. The liquid music. The silver brain. Trans-parent. (See figure 14.)

Figure 14. The World

(death)

1.
One of my deaths is still stuck in the body of a child.

                                                           2.
One sits in a strange window reading Schopenhauer.

                                   3.
One of my deaths is silly. One of my deaths
Knows everything there is to know about fish,
How some are dazed, how some are whimsical.

4.
                              I carry a burning book
                              Into my own death.
                              It has this poem inside it.

                  5.
              One of my deaths is a secret. One is studying Zen.
              One is an aphid silently eating
              The rose of my sleep.

                        6.
On a street corner death sells pictures of itself.
On tv Sam Donaldson is interviewing death.

                  7.
One of my deaths is diffident;
One is musicless; one is handsome,
Burning the air with his looks.

                                                    8.
Death carries a complex gadget. Light flows out
Of death's bright hands. It is as lovely as ice.

9.
One
Of
My
Deaths
Is
Retroactive.

10.
Death glows in the minds of saints and generals.

11.
One of my deaths   is writing a poem
That will not contain me.   He has fallen
In love with Emily Dickinson. One is whole.
One is old and sings of   owls.

12.
One has visited South Africa. One of my deaths is in the body
Of a woman. One is trying to keep warm. One
Of my deaths is clumsy; another is keen.

13.
                    Death bursts into glass.

14.
One of my deaths loves Matisse;
Another loves Brueghel's
Stumbling scenes.

15.
One of my deaths smells like a candle.

16.
One of my deaths is a nation
That feeds itself to children,
That exports itself to stars.

17.
Death is wearing
The uniform
Of the last person
We put in charge.

18.
One of my deaths is my dinner.
One of my deaths sends me a map
Showing me how to get to where
He is waiting. Another has
Forgotten what I look like.
Then suddenly remembers.

(food)

The starving child shatters. We eat so others starve.

To be beautiful is to be invisible. I offer you recipes for light,

For excuses, for delicacies of air, holes.

The sibling keels over and the world continues. It is always

Our food. (   ) Death holds our hands and we grow tired,

Amazed at how we are no longer amazed.

What is us separates and moves off, bits, scattered bits of us,

To form other things that no one will recognize as us.

I am so thin I am musical. Choreographed,

Terrible, foreign, I am a slice of air. The world

Moves through me like a crack. (   )

We can feel the emptiness in our mouths. The stream

Like a shoelace is being pulled through the forest.

Whatever happened

To meaning? Shadows stain the ground and recall us.

The starving child stares at us through the holes in its eyes

While we consume Elvis and shopping malls, while we eat

The light from the brains of the animals around us.

I am eating the white paper with (

) ink. I am eating the margins. I am eating

The homes of the homeless, the cries of laboratory animals,

The cries of women when they send their wombs to war.

How to understand the body? Corpulent with colors.

Sometimes strict, lean, sunken, saying goodbye with faded eyes.

Maybe words(   ) can change

The surface of a thing. Maybe our hunger

Can change the sky. I suffocate in the light

Of tv game shows, working on the right answers.

The right answers. I keep talking in a blue language.

My brother lives behind a new face. My father presides

Over a funeral of bees. There he is apologizing

For his madness. I say, "Hey, look..."

(   ) We keep

The starving child starving even though we don't want to.

Hunger cuts open the child's mouth. Always there is the chance

We can learn to speak

The way a tree speaks. Suddenly. My mother is old.

I want to touch her face. Though I know it will

Fall away or smudge or tear. Though I know

It will ache the way glass must ache the moment

It cracks. Her blue, blue face. (   )

The stream is anorexic. Food is political.

I don't want you to eat me the way I ate your house.

Something says feed me. I hear it at night in the goose pen,

In the heart, in the touch. I need help to bury this child.

Chalk, clay, ice cubes, (   ) plaster, dirt, paper. I am licking

The ink before it dries on the page. Paint chips.

Eating the pattern off the platter of my brain. Eating

Ideas, sawdust, zeros. My father is eating the world news.

My mother eats Latin. My sister is eating the album with the

Pictures of us choking. Styrofoam, sunlight, the sounds

Of a saxophone. The inside and outside blur. (

) My brother turns into my dead uncle.

I eat my own death and it tastes sweet like a shed full of bees.

I am eating blue, eating porcelain, swallowing time.

Maps. Pockets. Bottle caps. Innuendo.

I drink the light from a (   ) diamond. Listen,

You can hear the child starving. I remember how

My daughter first discovered the world with her mouth,

And now I must do the same. Eventually, we are

Captives of what we know, so we must know less.

The starving child aches. The ochre skin. The swollen

Tongue. The hole is getting bigger. My eyes piglike.

Everything is mouth. The air is violet, bloated with itself.

I eat meat. I eat stars. I eat the mind

Of my teachers. (   )

My room is a reliquary. I eat pheasant. Fish.

I eat the homes of animals, cans of soggy chemicals,

The entire alphabet. A hole is building itself around me.

If you love your mother you will eat.

Wallpaper. Glass. Doorknobs. You will eat the dust, the lamp.

You will eat tricks of the shimmering mirror. I eat sex

From cheap novels, gorge myself on the sweetness of the air

Around a woman's body. God is always hungry, sliding

Away, everything sucked into his joyless light. I keep

Receiving the picture of the child we are starving.

We have taken away its food and given it cash. We

Have taken away its land and given it cracks.

The Colonial Mind. We eat so others starve.

Our food is plastic. The body of the starving child

Is a burning book we cannot read. (

) The children report the boy has eaten

Dirt. The mother scolds him, saying, "Why did you eat dirt?"

"But I haven't. If you believe them instead of me,

Look into my mouth." The mother looks into the mouth of her

Son. And when she does she sees the whole universe: light,

An aging gray light, light flowing out of an extinguished

Star; constellations; factories manufacturing a vagueness,

An intoxicating vagueness; a river moving like a liquid muscle;

The sky touching everything; silence; trees; sleep; women

Marching with their flags on fire; impalas; waterfalls; voices made

Of stone; (   ) love; tears; stuff;

Hunger as big as a hotel. But the mother does not find herself,

Does not find her music in his mouth. (   )

And the starving child sits down beside us. My family

Gathers around a banquet of sweetness and silver. The pupils

Cracked, the esophagus crumbled, the starving child makes

Sucking sounds. I eat (   ) my own eyes in order

To see. I eat my mouth(   ) so I can sing.

I eat the maps to where we've been going. And when I look up

From my words (

) no matter how many I write (no matter how much I love)

The starving child (   ) still serves our dinner.

(love)

We are reading a burning book called love.
Word-nectar. Lips. We touch
The dreams we've hung inside our bones—
Light inside a chandelier.

....

The past is slow moving. It touches the present,
Brushes against it like breath, disturbs it benignly
Until it is gone.

....

We do the dance of the Original People—
Bodies spinning until we become wolves
Or crows or people capable of opening up
Our own heads.

....

The world is sending us part of itself,
Opaque islands with geese and stars, collections
Of indecipherable sensations that we have
To fit together or lose.

....

Our dance touches the air and opens it
All around us. You are my mouth mother.
You are the mother of this dance.

....

We dance with the planet, with the trees,
With the sun. Animal shadows around us.
We reinvent a collective self with the imagination:

....

enigmatic centerless flowing

....

We write this world
With words that have sat
In our mouths
A very long time.

....

The History of Dance: those dark bodies filled the wounds
Of air, and the temple dancers in Bangkok tilted.
The Sun Dance. The Flamenco. The minuet.
The *Danse basse.* Memory turned into motion.
The secrets of the body spilling in the air.

....

You are like a new word that has entered an ancient
Vocabulary. Undisturbed for centuries,
The whole collection of words is suddenly shaken,
Every word alive and altered
Because this new word has started a fire.

....

Imagine Nijinski those last 32 years
Talking to God when God wouldn't listen
Because he only wanted to hear Nijinski's
Body again, the leap of it, suspended, forever.
And then the drop like a diamond,
Like the weight of a significant idea.

....

Root-dance. Pearl-dance. Splintered-dance.
Healing-dance. Dust-dance. Seed-dance.

....

Why the rhythmic flow of the electron? Why
The resurrection of the dismembered body?
Why the small bones of our dancing?

....

The world is an immense message that we
Cannot decipher because we carry it inside us.
The way the sun is angled the leaves
Are catching fire at our feet.

....

Our dance replaces the air around our bodies,
The most velvet parts. Radiance.
A fire left in our shoes.

....

If we don't love, we dance with death.
The tangled dance. The poison-green dance.
The dance that eats the air. Thorn dance.
Plague dance. Crack dance.
The nothingness dance that stumbles out
Of our hearts. The dance where we sell
Death to the stars. When we walk
Outside we watch
The birds reach for the sky with our hands.

....

Addicted to risk we dance naked for hours,
Piled into one anothers arms, all flesh and fat,
And we dance only and only dance around
A soft mound of tossed pasts.

....

We want the cloudy whisper of the animal brain,
The clocks buried in the hypothalamus,
The dreamwork of the body. The meat of long kisses.
The climax of diamonds.

....

Dance to the tune of the owl.
To the sound of water. Dance is our body
Remembering the earth, the air, the fire.

....

Josephine Baker could be seen walking her cheetah
Or sometimes a swan through the streets of Paris.
She would come in on the shoulder
Of a giant, one pink flamingo feather
Between her legs.
The wild guess of her glances. Her unbreakable
Blackness. A great beneficent bird
Lives inside her dance. Correct the shatteredness.
Her beauty explodes.

How easily we cling to lost memory—genocide,
Culturecide, the matricidal wounding of the planet.

Dance is the way we pronounce our bodies;
Love is when the body breaks into song.
An emancipatory dance that rips the feet out of the grave,
The dark bodies filled with dancing.

I've watched my daughter dance, delirious, primitive,
Intuitive, a dervish merged with the world, all the
Blossoming stuff. And the music makes her visible.
Her body is all language, a meadow of consonants and Vowels.

She choreographs the air around her,
The self spinning out, becoming other, becoming star,
Making the air conscious.

Dance of dialogics. Dance of opposition.
Dance of resistance and identification.
Brain-music. Blood-music. A fire made of our footsteps.

....

The heart must crawl back inside
The things of the earth—or we die.

....

Confluent lovers. Chiasmatic lovers.
To resexualize the body against genital tyranny.
Body dance. Mind dance.
To dance with the animal under a shocking red moon.
To dance with the other in the interaction
Of linguistic textures.

....

The waterfall of our bodies: feet and thighs
And hips. Our navels touch.
A firefall of flesh.

....

The Yoruba have a ceremony— the Gelede—
Where men dress as women and dance for them
To show admiration and acknowledge their power.
I dance for you and vanish in the burning.

....

Our bodies burst into flame.

....

The stars make love to light
As we do our final dance
In this our final womb.

(light)

leide ferreira flies to her mother
with a mouthful of light. the people

(drawn to the light

are scrambled with joy. her mother wants her
to tell her why she looks like the moon,

(drawn to the light

but the moon gets caught in the house of her
daughter's head. and leide's old dusty father

(drawn to the light

dances like a chicken in the yard while the word
luna flashes in his daughter's mouth.

● ● ● ● ● ●

cannisters of cesium 137 had been
cracked open like the chests of revolutionaries.

                                  phototropism)

it was brilliant. it was as if someone had dug out
the inside of an ancient god. the people rubbed

                (words

it on their bodies, their thin limbs;
they brought it into their homes, their beds.

                    trapped in the

a woman in the tumult rubbed white in her hair.
six-year-old leide ferreira ate it—

story)

licked light from her lips. at first
she thought she was swallowing silk—

(words

it entered her so delicately. a crowd gathered
around the girl with the star in her belly.

              trapped

the light poured into her glands.
when she walked she was the story of light;

        in   the   mouth)

when she walked she was the whole
dazzling stream of light.

                    (words born

the townspeople saw her flashing
past their windows. now leide's mother

looks into her gleaming mouth and leide's
old father dances like a wounded chicken.

• • • • • •

her brothers and sisters come to touch her,
reluctantly
at first, then with glee, scratching the light around
her.

(light falls

among the gray laundry and heavy bowls,
she stands like a sun in the middle of the house

on the brain)

with her brothers and sisters circling her brightness.
her insides feel like the luminous center

(on the tongue)

of a grape—wobbly, uncertain, translucent.
she is standing under a waterfall of quivering light—

(the cavern

her body not a part of what her body is becoming.
the local priest, fat and mumbly, wants

                                        in the head)

        to pour her in his chalice.
        her name is entered in the fires

        (light   brims over)

        of the burning book. at night her family
        can see things by her body that they could

                    (shell   )

        never have seen in the day. leide's light
        burrows inside the things of the dark house:

        (throbbing light—

        the cassava, the furniture, the rosary.
        leide's light lives inside objects.

                        liquidity—

        a statue of mary glows when she looks at it.
        the cesium becomes one of her eggs

                    an egg opening)

        that begins its sluggish journey to the place
        where it will burst, haunting her insides.

            (flower   birds)

the doctor looking at her face can't determine
whether everyone is seeing ecstasy

                            (stories

or pain—though he declares
her incredibly content.

of light)

she can't shut the door on the fire
in her ragged brain. lying like a sunset

            (words   are

in her bed, she is afraid to find
her final body. they cover her to keep away

                                    crumbling)

her blinding flesh, a silver river
under sheets. she feels the light

(stories

drill a tiny hole into the center of her bones;
she coughs up gobs of mumbling light.

                are impossible)

the townspeople can see the house lit
from within like a sacristy lamp,

(the genitalia of women)

and that one house lights up the village,
and that one village lights up all the rest.

● ● ● ● ● ●

a man with a suit arrives
saying her bones will glow for thousands of years.

(I   is

her life is a tunnel at the end
of her light. when the six-year-old girl

always   a   question)

from brazil is buried in her special
lead coffin, the crowd gathers

(parent   thesis)

and throws stones at the casket.
they probably don't remember

(where are   the mothers where

the esculent light, the fistfuls
of divinity, and even if they do

                              are the fathers)

they just don't want all that radiance
seeping into their lives.

                    ●●●●●●

somewhere deep
in this earth

            (words burn

there is dreaming
done in light.

                        between

somewhere deep
in this earth

            the parenthesis)

a child's body
is glowing.

(dreams)

I am reading a burning book
called "History."
And it says we are crashing
into things: events, suffering,
the light of incoherent stars.

Ritualizing time. Revitalizing time.

The maps of wrinkled rivers.
Cities we can never touch.

Things almost happen.

I have entered each book of mine with the very clear impression
that I was expected, or, rather that I had been expected so long
they finally despaired of my coming.

Edmond Jabès

I admit to wanting a sword AND a vision.

Judy Grahn

I am reading a burning book
called "Victims."

When the soldiers marched the Navaho
to reservations, they shot those who
were physically disabled.

At night the wolves howled.
It was because they were eating
the people who were left behind.

At night the wolves howled.

It is difficult
to get the news from poems
yet men die miserably every day
for lack
of what is found there
William Carlos Williams

I am reading a burning book
called "Child."

The sparking red eyes of the owls.
The chill. A child is trapped.

The eyes are turning
into dark events.
The mouth holds onto want.

This child.
This child will fall
apart in our hands.

You cannot go into the womb to form the child; it is
there and makes itself and comes forth whole—and there
it is and you have made it and felt it, but it has come
itself—that is creative recognition.

Gertrude Stein

I am reading a burning book
called "Time."

If given enough time everything turns into its
opposite.

The wars they say we won
are the wars they say we lost.

This perpetual narrative of the failed revolutions.

If given enough opposition, everything turns into
time.

I reach for a taste of today.
                              Audre Lorde

Poetry after Dachau is a barbaric act.
                              Theodor Adorno

I am a burning book
called "World."

The trouble is the things that are trying
to speak to us have to use our words.

My cells carry around the memory of
how to rebuild the world,
so if it were torn apart...

The trouble is the things that are trying
to speak to us have to use our voices.

A word can take the place of an object in reality.
                                   Magritte

The poet's business is telling the truth.
                                   Ricardo Miró

I am a burning book
called "Air."

Our words are filled with air.
Our words fit inside the air.

Our words are on the air.
And we are on the air.

The mind is vast
what we know small.
Do you think we are not all
sewn together?
                    Susan Griffin

I am a burning book
called "Dreams." Alternative lives.
Simultaneous.

I am dreaming of a big star
in a big sky, of a big star
in a big sky.

I am dreaming about the Senoi,

About damaged dreams.

I have put my hand inside my head.
Here.

You ask me to plow the ground! Shall I take a knife and
tear my mother's bosom?

Smohalla

I am a burning book
called "Burning" —to see
the fire that burns inside everything,

to see the children who wear
their father's suicide,

to see resplendence,
to see the stains of daybreak,
the exposed roots,

to see the inner parts of the throat
where the songs rub.

I want to rediscover the secret of great speech and of
great burning.

Aimé Césaire

I am a burning book
called "History."
It is so dark in here
I can't see anything.

All history is modern history.
                    Wallace Stevens

History, which threatens this twilight world, is also the
force which would subject space to lived time.
                    Guy Debord

I am a burning book
called "Body."

I keep forgetting what the body
looks like.

Branches strangle light.
Breath bursts.

Our clothes hate our bodies.

...to write from the body is to re-create the world.
                        Ann Rosalind Jones

"I" am reading a burning book
called "Music."

The music of ideas, the music
of genes. Egg music.
Sperm music.

The vibration of nothingness.

Music is melted architecture.
The rickety intellect.

Music stops.

Music is the sole domain in which man realizes the
present.

Stravinsky

"I" am reading a burning book
called "Dreamer."

A woman gives me her dream
as a gift.
One man is lying in two beds.

One of him is alive
and one is dead.

She writes on the dead one's forehead:
"You may speak. I can hear you."

A death's-head. The dreamer wants to kick it away, but
cannot. The skull gradually changes into a red ball, then
into a woman's head which emits light.

Carl Jung

"I" am reading a burning book
called "Talking Stone."

According to the Senecas,
all stories originated
from a talking stone.

Lithic tongue.
Chips of words.

Symbols appear to be of their nature unsatisfied.
                                        Wittgenstein

The more I see of these Indians, the more convinced I am
that they all have to be killed or be maintained as a
species of paupers.
                        General William Tecumseh Sherman

105

"I" am reading a burning book
called "Woman."

A song cage.
Pour me into the womb.

Having come from woman, it is
woman we must be heading toward.

Home.

Her language does not contain, it carries: it does not
hold back, it makes possible.

Hélène Cixous

"I found God in myself and I loved her fiercely."

Ntosake Shange

"I" am reading a burning book
called "Heresy."
I am standing in the blood rooms.

He whose vision cannot cover
History's three thousand years,
Must in outer darkness hover,
Live within the day's frontiers.
          Goethe

"I" am reading a burning book
called "Revolution." The dreams
of the oppressed are still with us.
The Presidential Palaces
are filled with ghosts.

To survive there must be
a revolution: dark female earth.

Wildfire.
          harvest   dreams.

If you can't dance I don't want your revolution.
                                        Emma Goldman

"I" am reading a burning book
called "Reading a Burning Book."

A woman is talking.
A woman tells her story.

A woman touches her story.

In her statements—at least when she dares to speak
out—woman retouches herself constantly.

Luce Irigaray

"I" am reading a burning book
called "Liberation."

Words are sewn together—
sword-words, womb-words.

The living things we find
inside language.

The ecology of consciousness.

A language for witnessing.

A line of peace might appear
if we restructure the sentences our lives are speaking:
shift from affirming profit and power,
question our needs, allow long pauses.

                                    Denise Levertov

"I" am reading a burning book
called "Fire."

Every story is on fire.

We gave the Mohawks
a gift of blankets
infected with smallpox.

We have to remember
or burn.

Light the fire so I can see.
                    Samih al-Qasim

My storehouse having
Burnt down
Nothing obscures the view
Of the bright moon.
                    Masahide

"I" am reading a burning book
called "Child."

The secret police
have invaded the womb.

The soldiers had followed along the gulch, as they ran,
and murdered them in there. Sometimes they were in
heaps because they huddled together, and some were
scattered all along. Sometimes bunches of them had
been killed and torn to pieces where the wagon guns hit
them. I saw a little baby trying to suck its mother, but it
was bloody and dead.

Black Elk

"I" am reading a burning book
called "Parent Thesis."
The mother is the mother
and the father.

Everything is born
between the flesh
of the parentheses.

I never acknowledge myself to be either man or woman.
Paramhansa Yogananda

But all living art will be irrational, primitive, and
complex; it will speak a secret language and leave behind
documents not of edification but of paradox.
Hugo Ball

Reading a burning book
called "Earth." The earth is calling
the world back to itself.
It is calling the world.

The world is the self-disclosing openness of the broad
paths of the simple and the essential decisions in the
destiny of an historical people. The earth is the
spontaneous forthcoming of that which is continually
self-secluding and to that extent sheltering and
concealing. World and earth are essentially different
from one another and yet never separated. The world
grounds itself on the earth, and the earth gets through
the world.... The world, in resting upon the earth, strives
to surmount it. As self-opening it cannot endure
anything closed. The earth, however, as sheltering and
concealing, tends always to draw the world into itself
and keep it there.

                                    Martin Heidegger

Reading a burning book
called "Future."

The Hopi prophesies predicted
the white man.
They said if he came bearing
the sign of the circle

he would live in harmony.
But if he came bearing
a cross, he would bring

sickness and death.

This is what is the matter with us, we are bleeding at the
roots, because we are cut off from the earth and sun and
stars....
    D. H. Lawrence

          Why do we drink or eat
anything else but fire and light?
          Juan Ramon Jimenez

Reading a burning book
called "Libre-ration."
The Australian Aborigines
have made a musical mapping

of the outback.
To make a musical
mapping of the body

of the mind, of the energy
that flows between places.

To free the book from its words.
To free the map from its places.
To free the fire from its burning.

What good is thinking, writing or acting if one's only
achievement is to continue that long line of failures, self-
destructions and fatal spells lasting from Jude the
Obscure to Antonin Artaud.

                              Henri Lefebvre

Reading a burning book
called "Dreamer."

A woman gives me a dream
as a gift:
A man is walking in a woods

and another man is riding a white
horse on a ridge above the walking
man. They meet at a spot

where a pregnant woman is near
death. The man on the horse
says, "You will learn the secrets
of the universe if you cut open
her stomach." The other man
kneels between her legs, looking
into the dark, into the mystery.
He says, "No. I would rather have this."

The man cannot literally have sexual intercourse with
the earth. But he builds objects, thrashing machines, oil
wells, huge metal missiles—designed to fuck the earth.
Man builds continual extensions of himself and these
have their way with her, the earth.

Eve Ensler

Reading a burning book
called "Sleep."

My mother carries an egg
like the O of an astonished mouth.
It is its own house.

The ending sleeps inside the beginning.
The world sleeps inside
the egg. The book sleeps
inside its burning.

Fire sleeps inside the earth.

My mother falls asleep
and dreams.

The world is complete.
Books demand limits.
                    Barrett Watten

When I close a book
I open life.
                    Pablo Neruda

CPSIA information can be obtained at www.ICGtesting.com
Printed in the USA
BVOW081607140512

290168BV00004B/4/P

9 780788 001468